FUNNY WILDLIFE COLORING BOOK

Large Size 8.5" x 11" inches
(21.59 x 27.94 cm.)

LOVE
Super GIRL
Yes
hello
hey
little Princess

LOVE
GIRL
yes
hello
hey
little Princess

.5.

LOVE
GIRL
YES
hello
hey
little Princess

LOVE
GIRL
yes
hello
hey
little Princess

.10.

LOVE
Super GIRL
Yes
hello
hey
little Princess

LOVE
Super GIRL
yes
hello
hey
little Princess

LOVE
Super GIRL
Yes
little Princess
hello
hey

LOVE
Super GIRL
yes
hello
hey
little Princess

LOVE
Super GIRL
yes
hello
hey
little Princess

LOVE
SUPER GIRL
YES
hello
hey
little PRINCESS

LOVE
super GIRL
YES
hello
hey
little Princess

LOVE
Super GIRL
yes
hello
hey
little Princess

.25.

LOVE
Future GIRL
Yes
hello
hey
little Princess

LOVE
GIRL
yes
hello
hey
little Princess

LOVE
Super
GIRL
yes
hello
hey
little
Princess

LOVE
super GIRL
-yes
hello
hey
little Princess

LOVE
Super
GIRL
yes
hello
hey
little
Princess

LOVE
Super GIRL
YES
hello
hey
little Princess

LOVE
super
GiRL
yes
hello
hey
little
Princess

LOVE
Super GiRL
YES
hello
hey
little Princess

Hello Spring!
Spring time!
Lovely Spring
Spring is here!

LOVE
super
GIRL
yes
little
Princess
hello
hey